ARlevel-2.4

FOOD

100 YEARS AGO

by Allison Lassieur

amicus
readers

2

Say hello to amicus readers.

You'll find our helpful dog, Amicus, chasing a ball—to let you know the reading level of a book.

Learn to Read

Frequent repetition of sentence structures, high frequency words, and familiar topics provide ample support for brand new readers. Approximately 100 words.

Read Independently

Repetition is mixed with varied sentence structures and 6 to 8 content words per book are introduced with photo label and picture glossary supports. Approximately 150 words.

Read to Know More

These books feature a higher text load with additional nonfiction features such as more photos, time lines, and text divided into sections. Approximately 250 words.

Amicus Readers are published by Amicus
P.O. Box 1329, Mankato, Minnesota 56002
www.amicuspublishing.us

Printed in the United States of America at Corporate Graphics in North Mankato, Minnesota.

Editorial Credits
Series Editor   Rebecca Glaser
Series Designer   Heather Dreisbach
Photo Researcher   Heather Dreisbach

Library of Congress Cataloging-in-Publication Data
Lassieur, Allison.
  Food : 100 years ago / by Allison Lassieur.
    p. cm. – (Amicus Readers. 100 years ago)
  Includes index.
  Summary: "A level 2 Amicus Reader that discusses turn-of-the-century food and cooking methods and how they are different from the early 1900s to today. Includes "What's Different?" photo quiz."
  –Provided by publisher.
  ISBN 978-1-60753-162-3 (library binding)
  1. Food–History–Juvenile literature. I. Title.
TX355.L365 2012
641.309–dc22
                                            2010039118

Photo Credits
Library of Congress, Prints & Photographs Division, LC-DIG-npcc-30821, Cover, 5; Library of Congress, Prints & Photographs Division, Detroit Publishing Company Collection, LC-USZ62-112763, 1; Library of Congress, Prints & Photographs Division, Detroit Publishing Company Collection, LC-D4-43104, 6, 20m; The Granger Collection, NYC—All rights reserved, 9; KEYSTONE VIEW COMPANY/National Geographic Stock, 10; Minnesota Historical Society/Alfred Miller , 11, 20t; © PEMCO - Webster & Stevens Collection; Museum of History and Industry, Seattle/CORBIS, 13; The Granger Collection, NYC—All rights reserved, 14, 21t; Library of Congress, Prints & Photographs Division, LC-DIG-npcc-31217, 17; Mario Tama/Getty Images, 18, 21m; Rob Brimson/GettyImages, 20b; Minnesota Historical Society/Harry Darius Ayer (1878-1966) , 21b; Minnesota Historical Society, 22t; Ron Chapple Studios I Dreamstime.com, 22b

1126   7-2012
10 9 8 7 6 5 4 3 2

TABLE OF CONTENTS

4/19/14

WHERE FOOD
CAME FROM

In the early 1900s, people ate what
nearby farms grew. But things were
changing. New inventions gave
people more choices. Storing, buying,
and cooking food became easier.

Storing Food

In the early 1900s, many foods were not packaged. Cheeses and meats sat out on store counters. Foods like flour and potatoes were sold in bulk. They were stored in big crates and barrels.

Food packaging was a new idea. People invented machines that made cardboard and paper packaging. New inventions made canned food safer. Packaged food stayed fresher longer.

MORE THAN
FRESH
because
first VACUUM sealed
Flavor-Sealed Ham reaches you fresher than fresh! Prepared by the new Hormel process, the ham is first vacuum sealed in the container in which you receive it—and then vacuum cooked. All the way to you, Flavor-Sealed Ham is *secure from the effects of air, temperature and handling.*
This new stride in cooking science results in another achievement equally outstanding. *Every last bit of original ham goodness is saved!* The exclusive Hormel cooking process retains all those natural Flavors, Juices, Vitamins and Tenderness formerly lost in cooking water and vapor.
A valuable reserve food—instantly ready to serve cold. Grill in 3 minutes. Bake in a quarter the time once needed. Flavor-Sealed Ham has no bone, no skin, no waste. It is all ham from end to end—flavorful, tender, fresh.
At leading stores—or write, giving your dealer's name.
GEO. A. HORMEL & CO., Austin, Minn.
Exclusive Packers of Flavor-Sealed Products
HALF SIZE 3 to 5 lbs. BAKES IN 30 MINUTES
HALF SIZE PACKAGE
HORMEL Flavor-Sealed HAM
WITH ALL ITS NATURAL JUICES
HORMEL Flavor-Sealed HAM
THOROUGHLY COOKED READY TO SERVE
WHOLE HAM 6 to 10 lbs. BAKES IN 60 MINUTES
ALL ITS FLAVORS SEALED IN

BUYING FOOD

One hundred years ago, there were no one-stop supermarkets. People had to go to different stores to buy different foods. Fish markets sold fresh-caught crabs and fish. Butcher shops sold meat. Bakeries sold breads and pastries.

People weren't allowed to choose what they wanted from the store shelves. They told a store worker what they wanted. The worker gathered the foods and gave them to the customer.

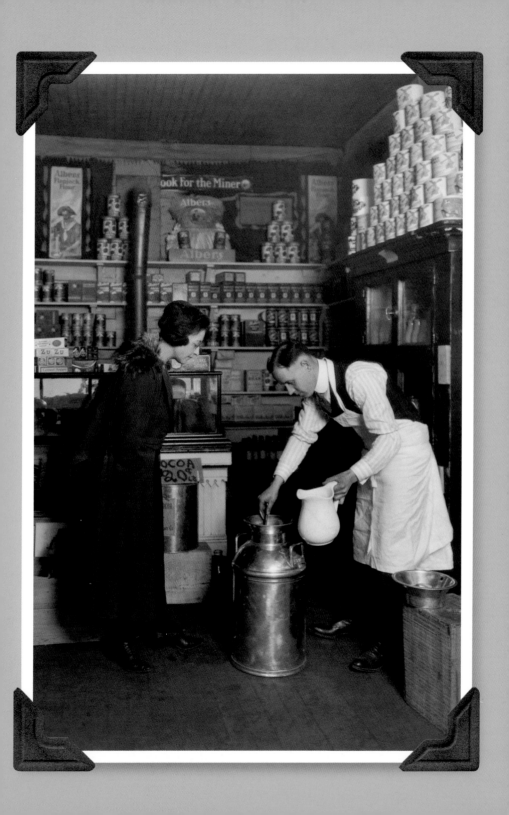

COOKING AND EATING FOOD

People cooked everything with fresh ingredients. There were no cake mixes. No one had ever seen macaroni and cheese in a box. Snack foods like potato chips did not exist.

One hundred years ago, there were no toasters or microwaves. The only way to cook food was on a big iron stove. Most stoves cooked food by burning a fire inside. It took a long time to cook a meal.

Many foods were invented one hundred years ago. The chocolate bar was invented in 1900. The first ice cream cone was made in 1904. Oreo cookies were first made in 1912. Now we can't imagine life without these foods.

bakery—a store that sells baked goods such as bread, pastries, pies, and cakes

bulk—a large quantity of something

butcher shop—a store that sells meat, where butchers cut the meat for customers

ingredients—foods
that are mixed together
to make something

invention—something
newly created that has
not been thought of
before

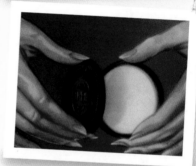

packaging—the
wrapping around food

WHAT'S DIFFERENT?

How many differences can you find between the grocery store from 1910 and the grocery store from today?

Ideas for Parents and Teachers

100 Years Ago, an Amicus Readers Level 2 series, introduces children to everyday life about 100 years ago, in the early 1900s. Use the following strategies to help readers predict and comprehend the text.

Before Reading
- Have children describe how foods are a part of daily life and where they get food.
- Ask about different foods they like and what they normally eat each day.

Read the Book
- Have the children read the book independently.
- Ask questions such as, *What do you notice in the photo of the old grocery store?* Point out details in the photos that are interesting or new to the child.
- Remind children to refer to the picture glossary if they are unsure of a new word.

After Reading
- Have the child explain how inventions one hundred years ago changed how people grow and eat food today.
- Encourage the child to think further by asking questions such as, *What kinds of foods do you think you would have eaten then?* and *If you went to a grocery store 100 years ago, how would the foods be different than they are today?*

INDEX

WEB SITES

Candywrapper Museum
http://www.candywrappermuseum.com/

The Food Museum
http://www.foodmuseum.com/

Key Ingredients—Smithsonian exhibit on Food in America
http://www.keyingredients.org/

Food of North America After 1500
http://www.historyforkids.org/learn/northamerica/after1500/food/